GERARD MANLEY HOPKINS
MEETS WALT WHITMAN IN HEAVEN
AND OTHER POEMS

. . .Shall we stand
Like two blades, bucks, a certain
Tilt to our heads and jut to our hips
To show our pride in sex?

. . .Godhead
There and manhood, one, One, won-
derful . . .

PHILIP DACEY

GERARD MANLEY HOPKINS MEETS WALT WHITMAN IN HEAVEN AND OTHER POEMS

WOOD ENGRAVINGS BY MICHAEL McCURDY

PENMAEN PRESS GREAT BARRINGTON

for
Emmett and Austin

FIRST EDITION

ISBN 0-915778-45-9   Quality paperback edition
ISBN 0-915778-43-2   Regular hardcover edition
ISBN 0-915778-44-0   Special signed edition

Printed at the Penmaen Press
R. D. 2, Box 145, Great Barrington,
Massachusetts 01230 U. S. A.

CONTENTS

AUTHOR'S NOTE

Although the following poems form a sequence based on the life of Gerard Manley Hopkins, they present a Hopkins the historical record may not always confirm. Some notes at the end of the volume supply information for those readers who might be concerned about the possible confusion of fact and fiction. I have not tried, in the composition of the poems, either to create or avoid such confusion. My attempt has been to negotiate between the poems' service to Hopkins' life and that life's service to the poems. I hope that the spirit of the Fr. Hopkins who lived from 1844 to 1889 can get comfortable between the lines of these poems, if not in them.

A DREAM OF HOPKINS

He came close, kissclose, naked and transformed.
His body lit, seemed so, from within. No
Priest nor poet now but thin—thank sorrow—
Man. Around his fleshglow fell shadows swarmed.
Then he did this: rocked. Rude. Like a ship stormed.
And pointed, one hand high, the other low,
At himself. Heart and loins. Pure pity. Though
In such selflight looked at once harmed, unharmed.
O, and was silent, not: not to say but be
He came a—watch!—word, what someone—who?—spoke.
Wrote? A one-word book to read, ever. See:
Skin, bones (scored, skewered) shine outloud: *We broke*
Down, then out in praise. Now keep a mystery
Bodied forth. Have, give us. And then I woke.

PART ONE

HOPKINS AT BALLIOL

(1863, Age 19)

SKIN

The library of Manresa House, a Jesuit novitiate,
September, 1868. A window opens onto the grounds.

MASTER OF NOVICES: What shall we do about this fellow Hopkins?
      He's an intense one, terribly divided against himself.

RECTOR: Do? I don't know there's anything we can do,
      Or should want to do. He's on the cross of himself,
      That's certain, but it might be a bit presumptuous
      Of us to want to take him off.

MASTER: Frankly,
      He worries me. He's cheerful enough. Bright
      As a tack. But did you hear he made a bonfire
      At his home in Hempstead the day he left
      And burned a stack of poems this thick? Everything
      He'd written. I think he thinks in coming here
      He's leaving the world behind him and entering
      The realm of pure spirit.

RECTOR: Then he hasn't heard
      Father Potter and his infernal violin. When will the
      Dear man learn to play that thing properly?
      Anyway, maybe burning was kind treatment for the poems.

MASTER: Maybe it was. Still, it could be a sign
      He's so intent on devoting himself to a world
      All Other that he forgets entrance there
      Can only be in, and through, the here and now.
      Maybe he's missed, for its staring him in the face
      Too clearly, the simple sense of Christ,
      That God in taking on flesh took on the world
      Itself, this one; that eternity
      Is in time. That's another cross-point,
      Where they meet. I think Hopkins
      Aspires to angelhood and wishes away

[11]

What he gives praise to God by being, poor
Man.

RECTOR: His friends at Highgate called him "Skin."
And what perfect irony, if you are right,
That they should have called him precisely
What it is he wishes to slip out of!

MASTER: There's also this: it seems that for about
Five years now he's written in a journal meant
To serve the purpose of disciplining his senses,
Especially his eyes; he said it was full of
Minute observations of the natural order, close
Jottings about leaf-shapes, bird-flights, and so forth.
The point is he came to me to speak of
Abandoning it. Hopkins believes it draws
Him away from his proper studies, draws him
Down. He spoke of the threat of the beautiful —
I swear he pronounced it with a capital "B"—
And of *natura maligna*. I reminded him of
The Ignatian exercises, the importance of the senses.

RECTOR: Hopkins' middle initial is "M." I gather
You think it stands for Manichaean.

MASTER: Joking about it won't change things.
For Hopkins, and others like him, nature
Is closed in upon itself, one-dimensional,
As if the finite were all separate
From the infinite. My fear is
Hopkins insufficiently loves Creation.

RECTOR: You could be right. Or perhaps Hopkins
Is merely attending, at the moment and with full
Focus, to Juan de la Cruz. It was excessive
Love of visible things he warned against,
Not love itself. Let Hopkins stop his
Scribbling for awhile, or forever. We cannot know

[12]

How his will and the greater will
Twine and work together as they work around
Each other. For example, look out this window,
At Father Chamberlain. He's got Hopkins in that tree
Picking apples. Chamberlain wants the ones
From the top. See how he points and urges.

MASTER: I hope Hopkins's spry enough to save his neck.

RECTOR: There's the end, for the moment at least,
        Of our division. Within that frame,
        Our two views of Hopkins join, like time and eternity
        Joining in a kind of absolute present, in
        The moving image Hopkins is right now.
        Look at him going up, up, up. One would think
        He had renounced us all, the whole imperfect
        Place, and was crawling his way skyward
        To find some escape hole at the top.
        But no, he's only going up to pluck the fruit
        Of earth, to pluck — how can he not? — himself.

No, I must not, must not now continue
Taking from God, by acts of love for
This world in the journal I told you of,
His time, what I have and owe, not own.
Father, give me permission for penance
To close that book against the flora
Of countryside and fauna of men's speech
I fill it with out of curiosity.
Curious. Akin to care. I care for
What I should not. The trees take me
Into themselves. I wept last week
To see one cut down, but before
Drew it, line and word, but no good.
It is gone. I cannot guess it anymore.
And I will come after it and so must turn
From those poor pages, poems even,
Father, forgive me, and shut my eyes
To better see the light I, let me, live for.

No, no, you need not say it, I know
This world is His as much as that one is,
Time and eternity divide the mystery
Mastery of the moment, Being is
Here, Presence present,
But in disguise, wearing the world,
And I watch too well the wearing,
The mere dress, dross.
                         That cedar,
The great one on the walk to the grove,
Smells in the sun, its bark, but not
In the shade. And in the cedar
A pigeon, yesterday, a tiny crush
Of satin green clear, hidden, clear
As the head bobbed above the breast.
I love the sun-bark and the green light

My poor notebook would see me into heaven.
O I am windy, blow, would grieve a
Gale. Let only my silence be heard.
For me, for long, the Via Negativa.
Yes, I know Christ is the word,
But, see, he too went in the tomb.
On the neck. If observation were prayer,
The world's too wide, I need less room.

MATER INVESTIDA

(Editor's note: The following two items, a letter from Gerard Manley Hopkins to Robert Bridges and a journal-entry by Hopkins constituting the three pages heretofore missing from Manuscript C. II, Bodl., were recently discovered together among papers of the late Col. Andrew Hough Bridges, grandson of the Laureate.)

I

Manresa House, Roehampton, April 9, 1874

Dearest Bridges,— Do you think you cd. locate and send me a copy of Kerr's *Ecclesiastical Entries*? Our library lists it as missing. I'm told Kerr speculates that some early Christian cults experimented with a blend of sexuality and religion. Scandal put a stop to them (not quickly, took decades, he says) and Christianity went off in a different direction, veered angelically. (Now you'll have something else to hold against the Roman Church.) No doubt Kerr's aim is wild but I shd. like to see if he can help me live with a dream I was visited, invaded, by last week. I'll spare you the disturbing details.

I'll be on retreat here from the 12th to the 18th, but can receive the book after that.

Gratefully and affectionately,

Gerard

II

April 3, 1874

I must record it
Before I forget it, though
The memory shall only
Bring me pain: Christ, His Mother
Naked on a throne.
He the infant propped

On her knee.   Both of them crowned,
The effect would have been comic
Had not a lurid light hung
        Heavily upon
        Their bodies.   They looked
At each other, as they do
In various images,
But with some knowledge between
        Them too advanced for
        An infant and too
Ripe for a holy virgin.
Nor was the form of her flesh
Restrained but expressed itself
        Clearly and with much
        Emphasis.   Coarseness
Even.   How to describe it?
But of course — the exhibit at
The Victoria and Albert
        Museum!   Only
        A few days ago.
It must have slipped into last
Night's dream. Stone- and earthenware
Recently excavated
        From the bowels of Crete.
        One terra-cotta
Figure in particular —
A goddess, 50 B. C.—
Held me to it.   Her.   So much so
        One of the young
        Scholastics I took
With me commented on my
Rapt manner.   I overheard:
"Father Hopkins would seem to
        Have a new subject
        For meditation.
And other than Ignatian."
(The tone was respectful if
Puckish.)   She was roughcast.   Bold-
        ly inattentive

To refinement.   No
Less powerful, though, for that;
Rather, more.   As if all her
Great energy were released
        Through the familiar
        Way she addressed (touched
Deeply, was deeply touched by)
The raw.   Her several dear
Parts were too large for her frame,
        Pushed forward to tell
        Reproduction.   Fruit.
Were not too large.   Told truth.   Told
With so pronounced an accent
I listened, lovingly, as
        Once, in Wales, learned new
        (To me) from hillfolk
Old words.   Thick on the tongue.   And
Sweet.   So it was with Mary.
But no, she was no statue;
        Saw her breathe.   And if
        She didn't move with
Dramatic fullness, gestures
Dropping a brood of meaning,
It was because she didn't
        Have to.   (She did, for
        One brief moment, seem
To point, with the hand free
Of the child, at her naked
Self.   Or was the finger at
        The breast aimed beyond,
        Where heart hid?   Who knows
Which?   It was the quickest sign,
For the quickest quick.   And I
Asleep.   I missed.   Mother, help.)
        But how express with
        What stiff shock (shame? *what*
Name?)   I marked where heaven's queen,
Who bore Him whom alone I
Love (loves me now less and less,

Seems to, what loss, mine)
And who on high is
(Was where she walked) lady-thin,
Gave way to heavy, pendent
Fleshfolds, gatherings thickpitched
        Towards earth, godgraced, gross?
        Cannot.   Can only
Record one more, greater, shock:
The babe turned and I saw was
No longer the babe, was I
        Hopkins-faced.   And old.
        Or, rather, not fresh;
Experienced.   Above the babe's
Body.   (Did I shiver then
In sleep? I shiver now.)   Saw
        Too, as if as part
        Of that image these
Other images: myself
As substitute on the cross
And loved lover of the, well,
        Woman.   She was that.
        Rosa cælestis.
*Rosa mystica.   Rosa
Incarnata.*   At the smile
On his (my) lips, a smile one
        Enjoys who steals back
        What once was his by
Rights but since lost, I woke.   In
A sweat.   Prayed God grant me dreams
More pure.   If it be His will.
        I must soon burn this.

ANGEL HOPKINS

(Editor's note: The following, recently found among the archival papers at St. George's, Worcester, are presumably the notes referred to by Gerard Manley Hopkins in his journal entry for August 31, 1879: "In the evening I preached on angels, but have misplaced the notes." The fragment of a letter from Hopkins to Robert Bridges, dated a day before the journal entry, and abandoned after less than a paragraph, appears overleaf. The fragment is reproduced below as an addendum.)

1.   The notes

To be or not an angel is the question.
Not that we could, but want to. Want wings
To flee the flesh-fall, all time to hover
So high sheerest feathers would weigh.
But Christ was no angel, dragging his body
Everywhere, up onto the cross even, even
With the rest of us, that low, level
With lust, but broadest such, for the narrow
Earth (who can, so cramped?), so doomed to sorrow.
We wrestle, then, like Jacob, though worse,
His had heft, could hand-hold, hurl down,
But ours, where is ours? Nowhere, is nothing,
Everywhere eludes, we tire who try to tie
Up fast that ghost.
                              If some angels appear
Armored, clank, or rich-robed, thank the artist
Who must do it so, lashed to paint, wood, stone.
But that a lie: so many angel-lies long last.
Best (that is, farthest from the truth) is this:
Angels once tempted by female beauty,
Not sexless, looked down from heaven at her,
Woman's locks, liked, love-locked, and quick
Begot children on her. Thus, to this day,
Women in church cover hair, their lure and trap.
The truth is angels are not so romantic,

Are (dare we say it?) boring. How could they be
Anything else? All day never to draw breath,
Nor feel the fire, inside, out, skin, soul,
The beautiful burn. Yet, we wish to be one,
No, yearn.
                    Weary, beware the temptation
Of angelhood. Fear to disappear. Envy
Not the lack-bodies. We fly better here who
Hug the ground, because God gave us his Son
(Sun, that fire, cross-fire, where we're caught, kissed),
As Word, world, whirl of atoms from Adam
To us, than they who free of gravity
Fight no force with counterforce to — whoops! — rise.
In heaven, though like them, we shall not be
Angels. Shall have our histories with us.
Then the poor angels shall look piteously
Thin, not to believe, but man fat with his
Past on earth, entirely credible.

2.   Addendum

Dearest Bridges,
                    I fainted yesterday.
Fell. It felt a little death. Did I smile
Going down, I wonder. I fast. Would lesson
(Lessen?) my body, whose role is rebel.
It will not not will, courts killing — I mean,
Being killed. And weep. Easily now. Saw
Riding wind a lark and for no reason,
Its beauty, height, or flaw, sobbed. Like a widow
Lost his body and would lose hers. We'd
Rob ourselves to keep from being robbed.

HOPKINS UNDER ETHER

During a six-week period he visited the dentist no less than eight times.
— Alfred Thomas, S.J., *Hopkins the Jesuit*

Ether, when sufficiently diluted with air, stimulates the mystical consciousness in an extraordinary degree.
— William James, *The Varieties of Religious Experience*

1.

Yes, Doctor, yes. *Breathe deeply.* Breath my memento mori.
Inhale, exhale, in . . . Hail, He comes (see there!) on a lit
Skyway, no, streak of lightning, with bright foot rides it
Down, balancing, as on a wire, but wider, and in full glory
Because — can it be? — the lightning is each step a spirit
Leaps to life, look, to bear (give walkroom to) Him, its
    whole history
Not long, mere touchtime, such honor. (O but how He bore, he-
el and toe, down that last soul!) What? Now I? Must I submit?

I must. I see now I too am part of that bolt, streak,
Stroke, my turn now come, to be the means he travels by,
Who grinds His being, up, from my pain, Whose foot
    tells Love and Law.
But now — no! — He would turn, sharply, strains to, till I go weak
To think of, feel, that weight willing a new course, then die
Into no God. Only the doctor, smiling, and, athrob, this jaw.

2.

To the Reverend John Henry Newman

Your kind query as to my welfare,
Personal, Jesuitical, poetic,
Arrived Monday. Many heartfelt thanks for it.
    Somehow I feel I could not answer
    You any better than to tell you
Of a recent visit to the dentist. Yes,

The dentist. The toothache was incidental
        But not so the wonder I saw, felt,
        Thanks to the ether. I went under
And immediately there was a great Presence
Travelling through the sky, his foot on a bolt
        Of lightning as a wheel rides a rail,
        It was his pathway. The bolt itself
Was made wholly of spirits, in countless numbers,
And I was one of them. Each came to conscious
        Life but briefly, for the time his foot
        Fell to it, and only that the Being
Might proceed on his way. Now he was above
Me, I had the privilege of his burden:
        It seemed he was grinding his life up
        Out of my pain and then I saw how
He wanted to change course, bend us who were the
Lightning in the direction he was willing.
        I saw, too, my helplessness, foresaw
        His success. Flexible, we bent, ah
With such hurt, the most in my life, and thereby
Understood things — eternal things kissed by time —
        I am glad to have forgotten, could not bear
        To retain, would go insane. Can remember
This, though: the angle of his turn was obtuse;
I knew had it been right or acute I would
        Have suffered more, understood more, died.
        Did wake, though. And my first thought was, with
A press of tears behind the eyes, "Domine
Non sum dignus." He, that God, thought no more of
        Hurting me than a man does of a
        Cork when he is opening wine or
Of a cartridge when he is firing. Yet still
I had that thought, knew I had been given a
        Role to play for which I was too small.
        There was a residue from the dream,
Ideas, colorings of feelings: Divine love
Is nothing but the relentlessness with which
        God bears down to travel where he would;
        Great discoveries, great prices; and

[23]

The sufferer, the fortunate victim who
Acts as "seer" on behalf of others, pays in
      Excess of what he gains for them — like
      One who sweats his life away to save
A district from famine, with a sack of gold-
Pieces for buying grain, meets God, who takes all
      But one piece: "That you may give them,
      You earned for them; the rest is for ME."
So. Does that answer all your questions? No doubt
Not. Upon opening my eyes I saw out
      The doctor's window, a dull street scene.
      (This was in Portman Square, Doctor Sass.)
The common light shrivelled the sense of what I
Had witnessed, borne. I was a mere aching jaw
      Once more. So I traffic, or wish to,
      Between the two lights. Reverend Sir,
Are they one? I think daily of your role in my
Choosing this life and give thanks. Believe me your
      Affectionate son in Christ, Gerard.

PART TWO

BEARDED HOPKINS

(1874, Age 30)

THE BLOOMERY

The shop of Felix Randal, farrier. Bedford Leigh, Manchester, 1879.
With Randal is Gerard Manley Hopkins.

HOPKINS: I need a sermon, Felix.

RANDAL: Chains, axes, ploughshares, grabhooks,
Shoes for ox or horse, I can even
Forge a special shoe to keep
A clumsy hack from tripping on his own hooves,
But a sermon? You'll wait a long time
Before I hammer one out on this anvil.

HOPKINS: You can give me one by giving me
A lesson in smithing.

RANDAL: Father, you're
Not likely to make a smith. Your arms
Are too thin, you've the chest
Of a boy, you're not half the size
Of my striker, and he's only fifteen.
Praying and preaching is your work . . . though
Perhaps your preaching could be tempered
A bit by common experience. We all
Admire your words, the sound of your ideas,
But the theology they taught you at St. Beuno's
Is hard iron for us here in Bedford Leigh.
Iron too hard is brittle, breaks easy,
Is of no use.

HOPKINS: You touch me
At a point I often touch myself.
So that yesterday, when I was here,
And I heard you speak of "roseheads"
And "the bloom inside a charge of ore,"
I thought of other blooms and roses,
Smithing and spirit mixed in my head,
And I caught the seed of a sermon finding

[27]

God in a blazing forge, and a forge
In His way with us.

RANDAL: You'll not find
God in my forge. I've got charcoal
And, as long as that old bellows blows,
A steady stream of air all around
The charcoal, giving it that glow, but
Nothing else. I built the forge myself,
Brick by brick, fifteen years ago;
I didn't put God into it. I'd remember that.

HOPKINS: I think men take shape by fire
And hammering. I mean the fire surrounds
Us, God breathes on it, then lifts
Us out only to strike us,
Before we cool, into something
Closer to his idea of us. Then
It's back into the fire. He's not
Quickly done.

RANDAL: I've had pieces like that —
Over and over, to get them right. But
I found this out: too much work
On a piece is sure to ruin it.
Its inner bond collapses from the
Strain. All its tiny particles
Just give up holding on to each other,
The whole mass relaxes into weakness.

HOPKINS: There, you're giving me precisely
What I need. Some men are too many
Times struck, too often in
And out of the fire; man is sorry
Material to make much out of.
Yet there is a mystery here: the doom,
Dear doom, of success by failure.
Man collapsed is Christ on the cross:
Total victory through total loss.

[28]

RANDAL: Father, I think you've started your sermon
Already.

HOPKINS: Then help me finish it.

RANDAL: I've got a wagon to repair this afternoon.
I've got to forge hooks for the whiffletree,
And a kingpin, the old one snapped in two.
Factory-made. If answering your
Questions now means I'll get
That much sooner back to my work,
I'll help you finish yours.

HOPKINS: A few
Ideas is all I need. Some
Will generate others will generate more.
I'll soon have enough for thirty sermons.

RANDAL: Shall I start with the anvil or the fire?
My time is moving between the two.

HOPKINS: The anvil, for all its ferocious heft,
Looks like a home. Start there.

RANDAL: It has to be a certain height.
A little too high, a little too low
Is no good, I'd wear my arm out in a day.
To keep it from sinking from its own
Weight, eighteen stone, and my pounding,
It's mounted on a green tree trunk
Upturned in a hole dug down
To hardpan. Careful measurement ahead
Of time saves a lot of trouble.
This square end is the heel. What looks
Like a steer's horn at the other end
Is called a horn. One end's as graceful
As the other's squat. Both serve.
Am I helping you at all?

[29]

HOPKINS: It's important
I understand the anvil in itself
Before I convert it for the purposes
Of my sermon into something else,
The instrument of God, malleable man's
Lure, his love and loathe. You help.
You tell the text for me to translate.
And the fire?

RANDAL: This is the second fire.
The first is in the furnace at the ironworks,
Where the ore goes in ore and comes out
Iron. The fire is for purification.
The more slag left in, the more
Brittle the iron. Wrought iron, what
Smiths use, is almost pure iron,
The weakness burnt, and hammered, off.

HOPKINS: I am distraught I am not wrought
Enough. Nor iron.

RANDAL: What's that you say?

HOPKINS: Mere mumbling. Mad. Continue.

RANDAL: The iron comes from the fire as a bloom.

HOPKINS: "The bloom inside a charge of ore"?

RANDAL: The same. A charge is ore and charcoal.
Lit, and fanned to hellfire, it blossoms
At the core to cherry-red, the bloom.
That hot beauty is what I watch for.
It's removed and worked. In minutes: iron.

HOPKINS: I like the wonderful inversion of nature:
No blossom on branchtip, but inside, deep-leafing.

RANDAL: You'll like, too, if I understand you,
The word for the furnace: it's called a bloomery.

HOPKINS: A bloomery! I would like to live there,
In there. "Sir, you can reach me at
'The Bloomery'."

RANDAL: The second fire is here,
A shaping fire. We know by color
What it can do. From red to white,
The range goes by degrees, a shade
Difference and the job can be undone;
The dull red of a near-dead sunset
Will do for a cat's-ear on a shoe,
But you need a bright Midland plum
To get a point back on a ploughshare.

HOPKINS: What would you call that color now?

RANDAL: That? I'd call that the blush of a lady.

HOPKINS: What's it good for?

RANDAL: The blush of a lady?

HOPKINS: Felix, you're having fun with me, a poor
Priest. I mean, what job does coal
That shade do?

RANDAL: That will turn a rod
Into a ring. By bending and a seamless
Weld, you introduce it to itself.

HOPKINS: I wonder if in God's fire there's
A color for each condition of the soul.

RANDAL: If He's got a forge, I hope for
His sake He's got a striker who

[31]

Gets there on time. Where's mine?
I can't do that wagon alone.

HOPKINS: He
Has one, a forge, if fable, I feel it,
But no striker, doesn't need one,
Not with our help who strike the self
So well. With, I fear, less music
Than you ring. Did you know the sound
Of you two in rhythm can be heard
A mile away, at St. Joseph's? His deep
Sledge, then your light hammer,
Back and forth, like an argument
Of high and low. Of heaven and earth.

RANDAL: You hear more in my work than I do.
I hear shillings and long hours.
But no music. No heavenly sounds.

HOPKINS: It must be my habit of the Incarnation.
I believe, which is know, there is no
Matter that does not wrap the spirit's story,
That, worldly, does not contain another world.

RANDAL: One world's enough for me. Don't
Misunderstand me, Father. I'm
A religious man, but iron is jealous.
The carpenter can lay down his wood
And return hours, days later. The
Saddler stitches at a pace he
And not the leather sets. But iron,
Once the fire is put to it,
Has a life of its own. Obstinate,
Quick, touchy. You have to stay
With it, nor blink. I sometimes think
The iron works the smith as much as
He it.

HOPKINS: Here comes another smith

For the iron to work. Your boy
Just turned into the lane. He's taking
His time.

RANDAL: Jack? He always does. He's a bit
The fool, though he's strong and has an eye
For where to swing the sledge. He hits
With good effect.

Enter the apprentice farrier.

                    Jack, get in here.
The wagon's waited more patiently than I have.
Take off your hat to Father Hopkins.

JACK: Sorry, Father. I meant no offense.
My ears are cold. The wind wants
To blow me away, but I won't let it.

HOPKINS: It's just the wind loves you so.

RANDAL: Where have you been?

JACK: In my bed.
I fell asleep.

RANDAL: I hope you dreamed
You finished all your chores by nightfall.

JACK: I dreamed I was a master farrier.

RANDAL: That's one dream won't come true. You'll not
Learn to shoe a horse in your sleep.

JACK: Then my nightmare must go hobbling.

RANDAL: Father doesn't sleep when he has work to do.
He's here now to write a sermon.

[33]

JACK: To write one
Here? In our shop?

RANDAL: My shop. He means to
Put the anvil in the pulpit on Sunday,
To bring us up to heaven with it.

JACK: Father,
If you'll forgive my saying so, it won't work.

HOPKINS: No?

JACK: No, it's too heavy. Won't rise easily.
But there's a different way to do much
The same thing.

HOPKINS: What's that?

JACK: Hang a weight on heaven and bring it
Down here. You'll find it less of a strain
To keep heaven from floating away
Than to hold what's heavy up that high.

HOPKINS: If you dreamed that idea
In your sleep, I'm going back
To the rectory to take a nap.
There might be a sermon there
Better than one I could fashion awake.
Felix, I'll apprentice myself to Jack.

RANDAL: Then Sunday's sermon will need as much
   repair
As this wagon. Jack, get busy. Fettle
The hammers and hardies. And rake the fire.

HOPKINS: Thank you for your time, good farrier.
It was a double-time for me: I heard

The heart in hearth and the fire in flower.
How I envy you your days of making!
"Felix." Latin for "happy." Felix
At the forge. And — our fate, ob-
stinate man's, inspired iron's — in it.
But wait, I can't leave before you say
What "roseheads" are.

RANDAL: They are nails.

HOPKINS: Oh, I see. To strike the rose.

RANDAL: Just so.

A GARLAND
FOR G. M. H.

"I have long been Fortune's football and am
blowing up the bladder of resolution big and
buxom for another kick of the foot."

Hopkins to Bridges, 26 July 1883

1. *NOMEN, NUMEN*

"Tuncks is a good name. Gerard Manley Tuncks."
GMH from his *Journals*

I am haplessly hopelessly Hopkins.
What is a Hopkins? A series of little
Hops. Leaplets. Nothing sustained. Nothing whole.
Hobbled-kind. Hare-minded. What begins
Well ends one length away. Half-happens.
A plan, hope-full, for poem, or more, hurries to a fall.
A man breathes in, puffed, breathes out, flat. That's all.
My name (help!) spells me out: what's whole? my sins.

Ah, but Tuncks. Tuncks. I would give such thanks
To be so named. Sound sound manly single.
Blow well-aimed at a mark; thought an arrow thinks.
Thunk. Thud. Straight for God. Good. Nothing will
Do but dead center, the heart of the Triangle
's Word, Holy Name no silence (sh!) outflanks.

2. *THE DEVICE*

Felix told me last night farriers
Forge tools they use only once. For special
Tasks. A hardy might do but not do well.
A wagon wants a hole shaped like an hourglass
And Smith must godly make leap from his coals
The very means, single, a saint of purpose.
He never names it. But, finished, puts it aside,
Which, in time, disappears, as if it had died.

O, to be so anonymous, and pure!
Would I had leaped a moment from God's fire
At His call, but be no Hopkins, nor man
Even, only a being, thing, device, dream
No word has fixed, free, to fill space well then
Pass. To the heaven of forms. Ah, a poem.

3. *THE MAN OF CAPERNAUM* (Mark 2, 1-12)

Hopkins Prepares His Sermon for October 5, 1879

I am that man, too, the palsied let down
Through the roof. But only part way. I
Dangle. I sway. Above me, a hole the sky
Is no bigger than, and ropes, heads, my own
Hands imploring — Steady, Friends, I sicken! —
A mattress below, below that a hundred eyes,
Press of crowd, rude, wanting a show, their noise
Surrounding that peculiar silence. His.

Yours, Lord. It entered him and he, look, walked.
I ask less. Would merely go down or up,
To heaven, home, the heavy body drop,
Or a low place, footed, like a bright snake
Mindless of duty, a connoisseur of grass.
A child would cheer to see me (down here) pass.

4. COMIC HOPKINS

July 25, 1880, Liverpool

Dear Grace,
>   Here is a little comedy
Or not. Who knows? I gave my flock Judas
Last Sunday and got back — O, rare success! —
Tears. My own ran until I couldn't see,
For joy. Too soon. For today, when my Cana
Drew them out again — what? where's the pathos
In jugs of wine? — I doubted and looked close:
Sweat! Credit summer's heat, not mine. Or say

Christ has his jokes. Ha! And changes abound:
Water's improved; passion's the crush of sun;
And kiss turns to cross. But, alas, Gerard
Stays Gerard. A man awaiting the Word
That, once said, and heard, will leave him other
Than this, though always
>   Your loving brother.

5. *A WORK IN PROGRESS*

"Wooldridge is painting my portrait."
GMH, from a letter, 3/29/87

Now I feel myself fall freshly away
To paint. Wet oils. Wooldridge wrestles me down
To canvas. That high. An impastoed heaven.
Let the Holy Ghost blow on me till I dry.
The new me. I. Eyeful. The old body
(Dublin my crucible, my killer, my own)
Transfigured beyond time, its touch (or soon
So — I smear); become eternal (ars longis) day.

No starry night? its scatterfire and fine
Fever? Nor moon risen like a pure thought
Over the town? No, no. Nor spun riverrun
To mock fixity, frozen sight, insight.
Which death then: brush or hourglass? Ask Christ,
Who hung (framed) at their crosspoint, and highest-priced.

THE PEACHES

The grounds of Manresa House, a Jesuit novitiate at Roehampton.
Sunday afternoon, June 4, 1882. Robert Bridges, who has come to
visit Gerard Manley Hopkins, halts their walk before
a stand of peaches.

BRIDGES: Let's have a peach.

HOPKINS: No, no, I must not.

BRIDGES: Why "must not"? Do your superiors
Count the fruit? Does Jesuitical meanness
Extend that far?

HOPKINS: Dear Robert, don't you
Tire of being unfair to my brothers?
I have just eaten. Anyway, you must remember
The very ground is Romish here:
One bite of what it bears and you
Might fall headlong into the Truth.

BRIDGES: It's not that you have just eaten
Makes you refuse. I merely wish
To partake, with a friend, you, of something
Sweet, and good for us, but the ghost
Of Ignatius haunts us and scares you
From a simple pleasure.

HOPKINS: I'll admit
I deny myself, and that it's a habit,
But it's a habit willed, and renewed,
Not fallen into out of habit.
Nor forced upon me by the Order,
As you imagine it. My No is no
Prison but a promise. Indeed,
It is truer to say I indulge
Myself in denials, in rich refusals.

[43]

BRIDGES: And in paradoxes.

Bridges plucks a peach from a tree.

                                    I believe this is a
Rochester.   Gold with a crimson blush
Half-spread around it. It reminds me of
Your own "gold-vermilion."

HOPKINS: You have a good memory.

BRIDGES: How could I forget? When you sent
The poem to me, you said it was the best
You ever wrote.

HOPKINS: Did I say that?
Another indulgence.

BRIDGES: I indulge, too:
In Beauty, the idea of it, but, better,
The particular of it. This beauty.
Is it so different with you? You told me
Not long ago of your extreme
Sensitivity to the beauty of the human body.
This is another body, less noble
Than the human, and thus no doubt
Less beautiful, but ultimately
Of the same matter, the earthly paradise.

HOPKINS: You left something out. I added
That such beauty is dangerous.

BRIDGES: The dangerous peach! I think this peach tree,
For you, whether you know it or not,
Is the tree of poetry. You fear to harvest
All it offers. A poem now and then,
Yes, when all the lines of your life converge
Just so and permit it, but not to pursue
Singlehandedly, with the cold will of the artist —

As if your God (or your Provincial General?)
Might suffer, or feel crowded, elbowed,
By the appearance in the world of another poem.
I know that asceticism, that fear,
But, more, I fear that fear.

HOPKINS: Dare I fear your fear and make
It three-layered? No, it would topple.
I'll let you have the last fear,
But not the last word. The last word is
Thaumatrope.

BRIDGES: Thaumatrope?

HOPKINS: I have one
In my room to give your nephew Bertie. I was
Sorry to hear he's ill. You can take it to him.
It's not the usual horse and rider, but an egg
And chick. Now the chick is shelled,
Now it is not. And I, too, am
Two sides of a card. On one I'm in
Mid-air, as if leaped there, hot for heaven;
On the other a tree stands, fruited thick
But neglected, a human absence everywhere.
Twirl the card, though, and, behold, I'm
In the tree, burrowed in fruit, the hand
That held empty air now around a sweet
Round. Both sides are true, but the third's
Truer.

Hopkins takes down a peach.

                    So I'll eat with you, to prove
Nothing but that I eat with you.
The third side, after all, is an optical
Illusion.

BRIDGES: Due to the persistence of vision.

[45]

HOPKINS: And this peach is only a peach, no more
While no less. Don't take my taking it
To mean I'm renouncing, or even loosening,
My collar.

BRIDGES: I'll consider it pure, natural
Hunger. A host's handsomeness. Wholly.

They eat.

A SIMPLE GARDEN LADDER:

From the Lost Correspondence of Gerard Manley Hopkins
to Robert Bridges

Imagine: two men, naked, and a ladder,
Opened to a tall A. No place in particular,
Rather a dark abstraction from place.
The ladder, wood, worn, stands grounded, sure,
Yet yearns, by pointing, upward. The most
Remarkable the men, who ascend, descend
The steps, slow or leaping, acrobats, no,
Trans-acrobats, more than mere technicians,
Under the bar of the A, with bow, with crawl,
Between legs to enter and issue therefrom,
Or grapple, with the thing itself, hang, twist
Upon it, rack, riddle, and with each
Other as well, wrestle, to wring out breath
Or admission (even sometimes separately
With only, alone, earnest, themselves), sweat
All through this their shining badge. How lit?
Imagine this, then, Robert, and you have
My dream of nights ago. Or some of it:
There were innuendoes, shades and auras.
It stays and stays, as if not yet am I awake.

Who were they? Wild they were. In weak moments
I meditate upon those men, their ladder. Was it
Theirs? Possession by torment? It was, too, a
Tool. Whose, though? Another's they use, uses them?
Jacob and Esau, yes. But Esau saw no ladder.
Nor did they wrestle, only Jacob with
An angel. These took the place of angels,
Trafficked the vertical, heaven to earth
And reverse, yet wcre most clearly men, sexed,
No denying that. Their parts both were and were
Not part of the dream-dance without music:
Swinging freely in the sourceless light,

Seemed accompaniment, mere, for the moves
Of the whole bodies, and yet seemed also
What the whole bodies moved around
(Or the bodies, to be whole, moved around),
Circle-center to circumference.
                                    But why
Two? I thought of man divided, even
Christ divided. Between here and there,
The dark earth we take as lover, falling,
The sky, dark, if differently, if beautiful,
Appalling. But no, none of that will do,
Is too simple: these men of mine hung once
Upside down, feet hooked on upper rungs, hands
Grazing ground, so that direction was lost,
In going up they seemed to be going down,
Sky rode low under the flying earth, or seemed to,
I was as lost as North and South. Nor was one
Light the other dark in easy opposition, were twins
(Like Jacob and Esau), their fate shared, I woke
As together they lifted the ladder onto
Their backs (or was I still lost, and it
Was the ladder carried them away?).
                                    Dare
I, Robert, even for laugh, suggest they
Were we? At serious play between
Pride and prayer? Or in debate about my
Faith, the Jesuit ideal (you disapprove; thus,
As I, in my terms, mount, or would, you see
My sad decline). But their bodies were similarly
Trim; ours are no such pair: you, long athletic,
Show it; bare, I am poor, minimal, boy-bodied.
If I watched us, we were in disguise.
Whatever it was I watched was in disguise.

Still, I know this much: it was a simple
Garden ladder. To climb upon to pick
Fruit from a tree. In looking back I am surprised
It was so simple a thing. It seemed so much more.

[48]

Though I can't say for certain now, it it-
self might have been the very source of light,
In memory it feels so. Ladder-light
By which I saw the bodies of the men.
By which they saw each other and themselves.

PART THREE

HOPKINS AT STONYHURST
(1882, Age 38)

THE SITTING

1887. The London studio of Harry Ellis Wooldridge.

HOPKINS: O, it is a good thing you do.

WOOLDRIDGE: But I haven't let you see it, Father.

HOPKINS: I mean that you transform my body
Into paint. It needs transformation
Into something. Already I can feel myself
Falling away, freshly, to wet oils.
Touch me and I smear. Let
The Holy Ghost blow on me till I dry.

WOOLDRIDGE: Stop moving, Father. Unless
You sit still, I'll have more Hopkinses
Than I can put together.

HOPKINS: I have one
And give him to you. I'll cling to canvas.
My cross. I'll hang.

WOOLDRIDGE: But I don't wish
To crucify you. Only paint you.

HOPKINS: A crucifixion, no. A fiction, yes.
In some ways they're the same thing.

WOOLDRIDGE: Pontius Pilate as artist? Pose.

HOPKINS: I mean the beautiful betrayal
Of your work. For a few gold coins
(How much is Bridges paying you, by the way?)
You betray me to a sort of heaven.
A heaven of forms. I acquire there

A new body. In time, yet out of it.

WOOLDRIDGE: Isn't Dublin heaven enough for you?

HOPKINS: It is the only taste of hell
I hope to have. I waste. No doubt
I'll pass before the Home Rule bill does.

WOOLDRIDGE: Nonsense. You're quite youthful-looking.
Aren't our ages about the same?

HOPKINS: I'm
Forty-three. You must be in league
With the young poetess Katherine Tynan.
Only last week she told me that on first
Seeing me she took me for twenty.
I thanked her for the compliment but reminded her
Appearances deceive: my heart and vitals
Are all shaggy with the whitest hair.

WOOLDRIDGE: Perhaps in the portrait I can expose
That heart. Fix it like a badge
To the breast of your cassock.

HOPKINS: And I
Could be pointing to it? Like Christ
In devotional pictures of the Sacred Heart?
The Shaggy Heart of Hopkins. Blasphemous.
Anyway, Miss Tynan would never believe it.

WOOLDRIDGE: Dublin can't be all that bad
With Miss Tynan there. I wish I
Had a young woman denying my age.
I only have too many commissions.
And unless I stop talking soon, I'll
Be too long completing this one.

HOPKINS: When I first went up to Balliol
I intended to be a painter. My brother,

[54]

Arthur, the painter, and I still argue
Happily over the latest exhibits.
But I found that the higher and more
Attractive parts of the art put
A strain upon the passions I thought
It best not to encounter. I feared
(Still fear?) the human body, its
Importance to the painter as the first
And last stuff of his art. The nude
Man, nude woman as the very type
Of creation. Of the divine plenum
Put on flesh. If the star knot
At the heart of an oak tree can set
Me atremble, you can imagine how
In the presence of the beautiful matter
Our spirits wear, I would be lost entirely.

WOOLDRIDGE: Do I hear you correctly? Maybe
My mind's too much on this
Cobalt and the set of your head
But is it not your own body, your own
Beautiful matter, you said you wish
To give over, abstract yourself from?

HOPKINS: Oh my body could never model
For Apollo. The day risen. There are shadows
Stitched into my skin. Nor even for
Adam fallen. He was the first,
I feel like the last, man. Unless Eve
Would renew me. I'll never know.
Now St. Sebastian, that's possible.
The arrows already are there, in place,
And but wanting the eye to see them.
I feel them. I writhe. My body might
Just might supply a hint of that sweet
Invasion. Martyr-making. Though
Best for that (because younger,
Purer, more heavenly handsome)
Might be those boys I saw one

[55]

Summer swimming in the Wye (do you think
"downdolphinry and bellbright bodies"
Too precious? I have those words
Left from the experience and now must
Find a poem to build around them)
And haven't forgotten. They stay
Like an amulet. How pagan
Of me. Perhaps if I cannot
Translate into paint I can
Into one of those pure human
Animals. Or translate one of them
(All?) into (thank poetry) me.
Splash!

WOOLDRIDGE: Let's consider your splash
A dive into this canvas. You've leaped
The gap. I hope. I wouldn't have you
Hanging in midair. To fall
Who knows where. That's all
For today. Would you like to look?

HOPKINS: Gladly. I ache. This is worse
Than hours in the confessional.
                  Glory
Be to God for gifted hands!
You have me. There. All colored
And removed. I'm moved to see it.
What will my superiors say when I return
. And will have disappeared?

WOOLDRIDGE: They'll say
Hello. They'll see through your
Invisibility. Look, you've paint
On your cassock. You've become
Your own work of art.

HOPKINS: Or a spot
In that direction. Or splotch. Or not.

[56]

REMEMBERING ADAM AND EVE

Hopkins, Heady with Wine, Makes a Speech
At the Wedding of His Brother Everard
(May 15, 1888)

They could not live in it. You can.
The garden.
And it is what you enter now,
Where the two
Of them once spent the day dreaming
Some gay thing
Would happen to break the boredom
Of such time-
less perfection. It did. And out
They went. What,
Though, our first, and fabulous, parents
Had no sense
Of was the good fortune that fell
To us all
From their appetite. For when God,
As Son, made
Himself Man, put on poor earth-flesh
To bring us
All back home, everything turned
Upside down.
The garden, once outside, now *was*
Time (and is,
Will be). Divinity intersected
With the world
Raised that world up to a power
Past number.
That is to say, we didn't have
To move;
Where we were, thanks to Christ Jesus,
Became the place
We had to go to. So, welcome!

Such a handsome
Pair as you is the truest sign
Of our return
To ourselves. For the loss of green
Eden
Was the loss of green us: the ring
Of Being
Broke; mere disconnectedness broke
Out like
The Great, the deadly, Plague. Here, though,
Today,
When you two say, I do, I do,
You choose
Good health, God's health, the sanity
Of unity;
You choose for us, and them. They would,
If they could,
Thank you. We can and do. And wish
You well, flesh
And ghost. I see them wandering still,
Outcast, all
Naked, shivering, ashamed. Come
In, Adam;
Enter, Eve. Here is the garden.
Here. Come in.

ESSAYS IN CRITICISM

From the Lost Journal of Gerard Manley Hopkins

March 3, 1889

It was like looking into a mirror
Almost. Meeting Guerin in Arnold's pages.
Georges-Maurice de Guerin. Here I am,
In Dublin, dreary city, a Professor of Greek
Drowning in students' papers and the noise
Of the Irish, who think what's loudest is truest,
Yet there I was, too, at La Chênaie,
A mere twenty-one, a pure fire lighting up
My entire soul no less than the hearth-fire
Lit up the faces of Abbé Lamennais and his followers.
Such a circle! God's own. Its center
Everywhere, its circumference nowhere. And both
In Brittany, 1832, for dear, doomed Maurice.

He called it an "oasis." The world
At a distance. Beyond the lime trees, beyond
The woods. He had come to discover
What God intended for him. Letters
Or the Lord? In *le Cahier Vert,* a beloved
Green notebook of his, he records the talk
Of Lamennais: "Poor man has one foot
In the finite and the other in the infinite.
Thus he suffers." Next to this, in the margin —
How central marginal space can be,
As if we entered, always, the Holy
Of Holies through a side door, or crack
We did not even know was there, the great
Front door open wide, and languishing —
Guerin wrote, then underlined, "That is I."

Who loved literature, but loved it to the point
Love turns, as if it goes around a corner
And becomes something else. Once, late at night,

While consulting his green notebook by
Filling it up, he heard scratching. His. Heard it
As he never had before, an assault on
Silence. That great absence now revealed itself
A greater presence. It spread from around his
Pen, across the fields, and beyond. The light
Sounds he was making shrank, down to the size
Of the unholy, while seeming to grow
Louder. Became a flaw concentrated
At the end of his pen, which he lifted,
Breaking the flow, convinced a living
Atom slept in the crease of his page
And he, by noisily spilling ink,
Disturbed it. He joined the order

But not before passing final judgment
On the literary life. "A career
In letters seems to me unreal, both in
Its own essence and in the rewards one
Seeks from it, and therefore fatally marred
By a secret absurdity." His poems,
Letters, and *le Cahier Vert* were published
After his death. At twenty-eight. Young, yet
Not. He had grown so thin, consumed by self-
Imposed rigors, men joked they could see through
Him to heaven. Was he that first man his
Creature (who tells his own life story in
"The Centaur," Guerin's capstone) sees? Climbing
A hill. "Behold the half of what I am —
How short and labored his steps, who must be
A centaur the gods overthrew, and reduced,
He drags himself along so!" A masterpiece,
Arnold says. I shall not leave Dublin
Alive.
                              March 4, 1889

        I slept well. Feel much recovered
From my strange fit of errancy last night.

It was the late hour and I was tired.
Meanwhile the mirror has fogged. Perhaps because
Of the dream I woke up from this morning:
Guerin was stretched upon a casement-ledge,
In bright sunlight, and I knew he was like
An Aeolian harp, no, was in fact
The very thing, in human form. Waiting.
For a breeze. The picture of beautiful
Passivity. I do not know if the breeze
Blew. But I heard a music, or saw it,
Rather, rise from his body, like a mist,
The music, maybe, of his waiting. Or
The music of the absence of a breeze.
No doubt the dream means I must give up my
Dreadful will. Or that I should have practiced
The violin more. Or that I'm inside
Too much with examinations. Or all
Of these. Or, mainly, late at night, read Paul.

HOPKINS TO BRIDGES:

From the Lost Correspondence

Christ's body came to me. The thing itself.
It was upon the cross and in a deep lean
Toward me, kneeling maybe. Or the cross
Itself was tilting dangerously.
Could I, was I supposed to, catch it,
Him? Heavy — I could see that.
Chest wide and, a winded sail, full.
A gleam of oil everywhere, for strength.
Christ, he came close. What did he want,
Want to give? Me back my body?
But this one was manly beautiful,
A waist narrow for athlete-leaping,
No waste, nor mine. And yet, yet, a loan,
Alone, to him, my body, yours, ours,
And what he took was returning after
Good use (good news), no, best use because
The wearing made younger, fresher, flesh.

It came and came. A press. Airless
Almost. Take, take. Take back.
I was taken aback: saw there the whole
Man, cock even, Christ-cock, nor nest-
ed neat and tame on its two eggs
But aswing, with God-sway, God's way
This way, too, I saw, along the King's
Thighway, thew and muscle-string.
                              Knew then
Why this coming, for kiss, to kiss myself
Through him and thereby bless this bone-house mean
House I never mind except to pray away.
And did. Kiss the head. (God!) Godhead
There and manhood, one, One, Won-
derful though I woke in sweat and stood

Up. Like a schoolboy, Robert. I write to say
There is a theology of going hard
Our dreams (but not we, godly) dare.

Gerard

THE SLEEP

"I am so happy."
The final, death-bed words of G.M.H.

It is an answer, a going-into.
The soft helmet slowly eases over the head.
The limbs begin to believe in their gravity,
The dark age of faith begins, a god below
Draws down the body, he wants it
And we are flattered.
We are going to the level of water.
(Don't hold on. Drop fair, drop fair.)
This is a fine seepage, we think,
Seepage ravelling to a river
To set ourselves upon. So
What is the price of dark water?
Where is the weight going?
The body powers the vaguest of shapes,
Pilot-boat, the falls collapse
And collapse upon themselves. We hear them
In time and imitate them.
We would turn to water that has lost
Its floor, water surprisingly
In space and beading,
A glittering disintegration.

              Now, what was a bed
Rocks just perceptibly, this is a cradle
In search of a captain, the bone-cargo
Settles, the medium
Washes up over and across and fills
The spaces we have been keeping empty just for this,
The palpable black herein
Barbarian, riding us down.

              There will be a level
We come to, will we know it?

A flat place with, look, a light.
It is a guess as our loins give way.
Already we are forgetting
Where we were
And left from, the human
Faces like sunglare hurting our eyes.
Did we even wave goodbye? Yet could there
Possibly be someone here now,
That this going down
Not be so sole, and sore,
A cup, a cupped hand, a basket,
These forms of containment
Forms of Person
Where, when we're water, we're caught?
Listen. It is the sound of ourselves,
This passage: a breath.
We are almost not here
If we break up this softly,
We must be incomparably lovely.

PART FOUR

UNFINISHED HOPKINS, DUBLIN

(1889, Age 44)

GERARD MANLEY HOPKINS
MEETS WALT WHITMAN IN HEAVEN

An Entertainment

Scene: A swimming hole duplicating Thomas Eakins'. Six swimmers are posed accordingly. As Whitman and Hopkins enter, the swimmers go into motion. The effect is that of a painting come to life by the entrance of the two poets.

HOPKINS:　　　For us, Walt, heaven is a swimming hole.
　　　　　　　God has decreed it so.　We are
　　　　　　　To spend eternity here, beside
　　　　　　　And in these waters, flanked by the flanks
　　　　　　　Of naked young men.

WHITMAN:　　　　　　　　　　　　But you're
　　　　　　　A priest.　I can understand why I
　　　　　　　Should be here, my heaven on earth,
　　　　　　　In the arms of a well-formed and loving
　　　　　　　Boy, become my earth in heaven,
　　　　　　　But unless your order has replaced its
　　　　　　　Prayer book with my *Leaves of Grass*
　　　　　　　I could sooner count the drops
　　　　　　　In that pool than say why you're here.

HOPKINS:　　　Many reasons, I suppose, but none
　　　　　　　For me to know absolutely.　Who
　　　　　　　Put me here explains nothing
　　　　　　　Fully.　I once wrote to Bridges —
　　　　　　　That's Robert, the poet, who acted as conductor
　　　　　　　Between your work and me, the fire
　　　　　　　Leaped — that I thought no one could admire
　　　　　　　The beauty of the human body more
　　　　　　　Than I.　Still or in action.　Did you see
　　　　　　　That dive?　Fairfall?　And a poem of mine,
　　　　　　　Alas, like many others, most
　　　　　　　Of my gestures, unfinished, called "Epithalamion,"
　　　　　　　Celebrated my brother Everard's marriage

[69]

By drawing a scene much like the one
We've entered. "Boys from the town" with
"Bellbright bodies" frolic
In a river, the "kindcold" Hodder, while a
Spying stranger undoes piece
By piece his wear until, Adam
Again, he tries a pool close-by,
Splash, and swims, laughs, is lavish
In his gay grasp and waterloss,
His float and wet kiss intimate.

WHITMAN: You're the first pagan Jesuit
I've ever met. My pleasure.
No wonder that poem never saw
Completion. To turn material like that
Into a wedding gift would require
A miracle. You're not St. Hopkins,
Are you, yet? Unless a couple
Of the swimming boys wed.

HOPKINS: The dean
Or dell was to be wedlock, the water
Spousal love, and the flora
Relatives and friends "ranked round."

WHITMAN: And your brother and his wife? Two weeds?
Or rocks? Or would they enter and the bride
Startle the boys into hiding?

HOPKINS: I admit
To ill-conceiving. I was distracted
By God's plenty in the form of flashing
Backs, and hair that, whipped, gave
Worlds to space, balled grace.

WHITMAN: I like the pure version of your poem.
Stripped. The sacred sense of the skin.
But better I like that red-haired one

Who did the flip. Look out! He means
To soak us till we might as well
Get in.

HOPKINS: "They do not think whom they souse
With spray."

WHITMAN: You quote me before
I could quote myself. You know my work
Well. I wish I had known yours.

HOPKINS: My knowledge was scattered, partialpoor.
But I picked up much from hints. I derived
Whole meals from scraps. One leaf
Or a few lines of a leaf. So it was
With your twenty-eight bathers.
One glance and they grew. Into me.
And now my poem, your poem, and this scene
Grow into each other. They
Marry. Marry! Even to a watcher
In each poem who "unseen sees." And we
The watchers here.

WHITMAN: I watch, I watch.
And more. Let the voyeurs consume themselves
In frets.

HOPKINS: That's my music.

WHITMAN: Did you
Die from such discordance? Men have.
Age won me, but you're too young.

HOPKINS: The immediate cause was Irish culture
In the form of Dublin's corrupted water
System. Unheavenly. Only bacilli
Swam it. I contracted typhoid. The Irish,
Whose ambition, I noted, has always been

[71]

To say a thing as everybody says it
Only louder, were no doubt glad
To be rid of me. If a sneer drives
An Irishman to madness, and it does,
I so drove many. My five years
In Dublin, dreary city, were my last,
And sufficient payment for this holiday —
And another drenching! Into what faith
Have I just been baptized? Do I
Offend any Irish blood in you?

WHITMAN: I had a good friend. Name of Doyle.
Peter. But I'll not let him, or me,
Get caught in cross-channel firing.

HOPKINS: And cross-Atlantic firing?

WHITMAN: If this
Pool proves salty, I'll know two states
Meet here, to contend, and sign a pact.
Hello, England.

HOPKINS: Hello, America.
And hello, Mr. Hyde.

WHITMAN: Who? I
Am no Hide. I am Mr. Show. Mr.
Peel off the heavy layers. Mr.
Bare the heart and loins. These clothes
Will have to go.

HOPKINS: Button up, Walt.
You'll have all eternity to parade
Unmediated by art. The water will wait.
Hyde is our Stevenson's new creation.
One man's secret self. You
Are mine. I told Bridges so:
"I always knew in my heart Walt

Whitman's mind to be more like my own
Than any other man's living."

WHITMAN: Why not? The mother country watches
From a distance her son. Or daughter?
I always thought I would have made a great
Mother myself.

HOPKINS: I agree. Your hair
Is mother-hair. Womb-white.
Long as moonlight trailing earth's
Shoulder. But I went further, said
(Heaven seems to perfect the memory!)
"As he is a very great scoundrel,
This is not a pleasant confession.
And this also makes me the more
Desirous to read him and the more
Determined I will not."

WHITMAN: "Scoundrel"?
Do I have to put up with an eternity
Of insults? I'd rather be ignored in hell.
I never liked priests, except a few
I met in the Civil War. When they saw
Me at bedside, the sick and dying
Pressed against my bosom, they forgot
What they'd heard about my book. That is
To say, my life. But they weren't Jesuits,
And they weren't English. My work had friends
In England, some as true or truer
Than any at home, and I admire
Your queen (America needs a queen
To lead her, we've had enough of
Fathers, Father) but fresh and open
Spaces let my book breathe,
And that means it doesn't survive
Tight collars well. See this neck?
Sunburnt. Airbathed.

[73]

HOPKINS: If I did not
                  Embrace you, it was from too much love,
                  Not lack of it.

WHITMAN: Don't get Jesuitical
                  With me. I'll drop you in the pool,
                  Robe and all. Roughhouse is American.
                  You're half my age but thin and from
                  The looks of you bird-light. Does every
                  Body here shrink so? I bet
                  You gave up eating the earth one Lent
                  And forgot to resume.

CHORUS OF SIX SWIMMERS: Throw him in,
                  Throw him in!

HOPKINS: Don't do so
                  Before hearing more. Looking at you,
                  At your poems, at the idea of you
                  I constructed, I felt I was looking
                  Into a mirror, one fogged no doubt
                  By a passage across the sea, but there
                  I was. I thought I looked good
                  In American garb, American gab.
                  The Society's secret: Gerard Manley
                  Whitman.

WHITMAN: I'll admit to envy
                  Of your middle name. Walter Manley,
                  Drop an "e" or not, would suit
                  My design. The brotherly curl of leaves.

HOPKINS: I know it suits. Gentlemanley.
                  You give new meaning to that term so
                  Important to me and my countrymen, there
                  On your American frontier.

WHITMAN: Brooklyn

Isn't in California, but I'll accept
The compliment. Maybe. If your black
Folds aren't hiding an edge to your words.

HOPKINS: My sympathies, though crossed with fear's fine
Hatches, are deep. "Long live the weeds
And the wilderness yet."

WHITMAN: Has that no edge?
My book's *Leaves of Grass*, not *Leaves
Of Weeds.*

HOPKINS: I mean refinement soon
And dangerous to its own achieve marks
No longer where it walks. Wallows.
Sinks. Will disappear the sooner
For facing away. To rare air.
As these lads, raw, throw themselves
In, and down, they rise. To take
The rarest air, because it hugs
Gravely — gulp — home. I mean
A lost commandment is, Thou
Shalt not murder Adam.

WHITMAN: But?

HOPKINS: But what?

WHITMAN: You said you once vowed not
To read me. That murders Adam. I
Fall. Would you murder out of love?
You haven't told me all.

HOPKINS: I would
Only dress him, to address him,
In distance, or the light wear of measure,
Or even great fronds from his own
Garden, great comfortable cloaks

[75]

Of green in which he could be seen
Anywhere, and be welcome, for to look
On him as he is, cloudclear and hot-
ly handsome, is to try to stare
Down the sun. Or say: too close
And we die. I keep him away
Just so far, to keep him by.

WHITMAN: Enough.

HOPKINS: Wait, Walt, what
Are you doing?

WHITMAN: Going for a swim.
I've had enough of your ungenerous
 And squeamish, slippery, simply bad-
Mannered ways. You're the barbaric
One here. My yawp was a love-call,
Amatory, adhesive, on wing for a new
Order, a new man, unafraid
Of the universe, parts and whole. Including
My parts. But you preach distrust
Of brother for brother. I'll shed these
Constricting cloths, loose as they are,
Right now. And when I drop my pants
We'll just see if you go blind
Or burn up like a piece of swinefat.

HOPKINS: Of course I was speaking metaphorically.

WHITMAN: Go dunk your metaphors, then. Here
I am. Head, shoulders, brawn
Of chest, rose-nipples I can feed
The world by, belly — slap it,
The sound is sound — electric beard,
Cock and balls swinging to a rhythm
Beyond numbers, the free verse
Of sex, thighs and knees, they take me

[76]

Over roads, and feet feel
The earth roll, the grass grow.
Now what do you say to that?

HOPKINS: "Glory be to God for dappled things!"

WHITMAN: A poem of yours?

HOPKINS: Yes, one
Of the finished ones.

WHITMAN: I present you
With my naked self, you give in return
A line from a poem. The difference between us
Couldn't be clearer.

HOPKINS: But I praise,
Celebrate.

WHITMAN: From a distance.

HOPKINS: How else
Can it be? Those "placid, self-contained"
Animals you've written about so lovingly
Are too sunk in themselves to rise up
Far enough to praise anything. Unless
You say they praise by being. Then who's
The Jesuitical one now? That rock, too,
Would so praise. Would you welcome life,
Or death, as an igneous hunk? I can't
Imagine you so static, hard.

WHITMAN: It's true I won't revise my title to
Hunks of Igneous: *Fragments Fallen
From a Man-Mountain*, but intimate praise
Is praise by doing. I loose my body
From hiding —

[77]

HOPKINS: "My heart in hiding stirred
                  For a bard."

WHITMAN: What?

HOPKINS: A bad joke.
                  We Victorians loved them.

WHITMAN: — and jump in!

CHORUS: Welcome to water. There's always room
              For one more.

WHITMAN: Glad to be here.
              To roll and thrash, float, flash
              And like a white whale blow spume.
              This is better than returning as grass
              Under a bootsole. I was right:
              Dying is luckier than anyone supposes.
              Father, you look lonely out there.
              And don't tell me your great love
              Of swimming keeps you out. I'm on
              To your tricks.

HOPKINS: I admit the water
              Invites. And I'll enter. But understand
              You are the poet of good health, of the robust
              Physique, the soul to match, I
              Never claimed to filter and fibre
              Anyone's blood. How could I?
              I couldn't filter and fibre my own.
              This cassock hides my third wreck.

WHITMAN: There are no wrecks in these waters.
              Only the sleek hulls of young men,
              And one slightly battered, though buoyant,
              Barge.

HOPKINS:　　　　　The Deutschland and the Eurydice were ships
That sank. My poems about them sank
Faster. But my body began shipping
Water from the start. I was always
Frail. Or made myself so. Once water
Was what I didn't have: drank
None for a week. To win a bet.
To prove my will (if not my wit).
To teach my body to submit. It
Presented me with a black tongue.

WHITMAN:　That's abuse of the body, not discipline.
I vowed in the middle of my life, forty
Years young, when I could see where I'd been
And where I was getting, to inaugurate
A pure, perfect, sweet, clean-blooded
Body. No fat meats. No late suppers.
The purest milk. Light meals. That
Was my religious act. You wished
To whip yourself to heaven. You whipped
Yourself to an early grave. Dublin's
Waters were just an excuse.

HOPKINS:　　　　　　　Viæ
Negativæ à la Whitman, à la Hopkins.
Mine led to fainting in the confessional,
A wasting of the little I began with.
And my body bears witness. As yours
Displays your history of health. I dare not
Be so quick as you to show it.
I love the human body, in general
And particular. As figure of the world's,
As matter to tire in the fitting dress
(Appropriate and close, it becomes) of a theology,
And as object, where the creation collects,
Moving, and moving, winded to mind,
In-spiritus. I love his, and his,
His, his, his, his,

[79]

And yours. But not mine. Mine
Was no friend. We fought. To the end.

WHITMAN :   Tom Eakins should be here. He'd
Patch up your quarrel in a hurry. I've
Been thinking of Eakins since I got here. Can't
Figure out why. He did my portrait.
A good one. Better than Alexander's. His
Made me look like a saint. That's your
Business. Tom painted a man.
I don't mean a sinner, I mean a mortal.
I was dressed, of course, but we joked
About his doing me in the buff:
Maybe sitting stiffly upright, formal,
Hands on knees, my beard my only
Cover. How fine that would have been!
America's new poet, smiling in his skin.
We both knew we weren't joking, too,
But didn't admit it to each other. So.
America's deprived of that vision. The Good
Grey Poet keeps his shirt on. But
Eakins pulled the loincloth off his
Male model and lost his job. The young
Philadelphia girls in Tom's class, who thought
That art was High Polite, screamed
And ran to the authorities. Then to their mammas.
Eakins remained steady through it all. Didn't
Blink. The artist's eye. My words —
You're right, heaven does perfect
The memory — could easily have been his:
"It is a sickly prudishness that bars
All appreciation of the divine beauty
Evidenced in Nature's cunningest work —
The human frame, form and face."

HOPKINS: Dear Harry Ploughman.

WHITMAN: Who?

[80]

HOPKINS: A man in a poem of mine. So named.
            "Harry Ploughman's Body" would have been more
            Accurate. Your words are like an abstract
            Of the poem. I studied him — muscle
            And shank, ribs, curls, and cheeks.
            Went as far as his "liquid waist"
            But not as far as Eakins. I had
            My Philadelphia in my Jesuit superiors.

WHITMAN: Recite it, recite it.

HOPKINS: I will, I will,
            But later. We have all eternity to
            Exchange poems. Right now I mean
            To test the waters.

WHITMAN: Then I converted you?
            You'll join my religion of brotherhood? Of
            Love, unchecked by the false god
            Guilt and his consort Fear, for the whole
            Body of creation as kin to man
            And woman? I knew some. Winsome.

HOPKINS: Know I also have a Philadelphia
            Within. And my collar, if removed, clings.
            It's just that the sun here, though never
            Not at midday height, and therefore
            Not sun, is hot. I sweat, like my
            Harry at his plough. I need a swim.

WHITMAN: Well, whatever the reason, it's time
            You got in. Maybe your doing so
            Will drown the distance between us. Who
            Knows? We might yet go arm-in-arm
            Through this paradise.

HOPKINS: We might. But not
            By denying our differences. Together we form

Our own pied beauty. All things counter
Cost only praise of them. I hereby
Shed robe, the rest, but not like a skin,
An earlier life outgrown and discarded,
More like wear, a way, gone
Interior, deeper than show.

WHITMAN: However
You spell it, it's Hopkins in the raw.

WHITMAN AND CHORUS: Hurray!

HOPKINS: If you're cheering for the singularity of my single
Private, as my hero Scotus,

SWIMMER No. 1:   — Did he say
"Scrotum"?—

HOPKINS: who loved Aquinas enough
To veer from him, cheered, charmed by, each
Univocal thing, any this
Distinct from the grand, omnivorous That,
There's a chance for us. Union
Makes no sense unless those to be
One are no such thing at all,
Nor likely to be, either.

WHITMAN: Union?
Is that a proposal?

HOPKINS: No, merely the prevailing
Myth of this place.

WHITMAN: Sounds restrictive
To me. I work best without check
With original energy. Your Society
Taught you well the habit of being

Prevailed upon, but my Society
Was Myself. I like room, not rooms.
Nor a myth I have to conform to.

HOPKINS: Consider it, if not just rumor,
             A kind of gravity. Which is honored most
             By failing to observe it. By, say,
             Dancing. Each step defies the Law
             Without which steps would be impossible.
             Or by, say, this:

WHITMAN: Look, he
             Dives, daring, into all this wet!
             Not practiced, but like an amateur, amat,
             He loves. There's hope for him yet.

HOPKINS: Help!

WHITMAN: What is it?

HOPKINS: This cold. It shocks. If
             Sweetly. You didn't warn me. But this
             Wreck still floats. For which I give
             Praise.

SWIMMER No. 1:   Did he say "race"?

CHORUS: A race!

WHITMAN AND HOPKINS: Who, us?

SWIMMER No. 2:   First one across
             And back's the ace of this swimming hole.

WHITMAN: Do you think that means Laureate, Father?

HOPKINS: Why not? Let the water be words and we
             Pull ourselves through to the last line.

[83]

Except I couldn't keep up. You said
Yourself you trained your body for years.
I only wished mine would disappear. Soul
Can't stroke. Still, if I can shake
Off this chill by a contest, I'm for it.

WHITMAN: Considering my age and your premature
Decline, we're evenly matched. Though
We won't set any records, even for here.
Who's to give us the signal?

CHORUS: Ready,
Set, go!

SWIMMER No. 3:   Oh, no, the small one
Seems to have swallowed his weight in water
Getting off. The old man's a natural.
Look at them have at it, each in his
Own way. One hugs the water, and it
Hugs him back. The other measures it
Out, portion by portion, his arms
Moving to a rhythm that cuts across
The water's moves. Syncopated swimmer!
Now at the turn he's recovered and challenges
The old man. Call them The Weather
And The Clock. They're neck and neck. Now
They look at each other and grin. In mid-swim.
What's up? An agreement? A thrown race?
No, just a momentary nod. A sleep
Or tribute to the other. But once again
Concentration's back. The water flies.
Weather's beard whips, but the Clock
Has a trick and holds his breath. Here
They come! It's hard to see. They're churning
Up a screen. In a rush, they arrive. It's
A tie!

SWIMMER No. 4:   No, it's Weather.

SWIMMER No. 5:   No, The Clock.

SWIMMER No. 6:   Ask
          Them.

WHITMAN: I think the water won. I'm tired.

HOPKINS: I'm sure I lost. I don't feel like
          The winner of anything. And I saw your hand,
          Walt, touch shore before mine.
          Not much, but enough.

WHITMAN: Manly honesty
          Requires I agree. But it also requires
          I confess I had an unfair advantage.

HOPKINS: The water's a member of your brotherhood and carried
          You part way?

WHITMAN: It is, and may have, but that's
          Not what I meant. I figured out
          Why Tom Eakins was on my mind. This scene
          These swimmers are his. We walked right into
          His painting, "The Swimming Hole." I saw it
          Once — *not* in Philadelphia — and knew
          I was home. I've been at home
          Since I got here. Even in your sheltered
          Jesuit's world you must have learned
          About the help to a team playing
          On its own ground.

HOPKINS: I loudly cheered
          Many a Balliol rowing crew at Oxford
          To victory.

WHITMAN: Then you know. And know
          We'd have to meet once more, on English

[85]

Ground, to be fair. These are American
Waters.

HOPKINS: You are a sportsmanlike winner.
And I can't argue about a painting I've never
Seen. But granting these are American
Waters, I'll also claim they aren't.

WHITMAN: Do you mean to say Tom Eakins has
An English counterpart? I don't believe it.

HOPKINS: I mean this scene, though earthly, is not
Earth. Did you forget, Walt, you died?
Welcome to heaven, like it or not.
Unless I've misread this place — my studies
In theology at St. Beuno's, Wales,
Could hardly have prepared me for such
An afterlife — your body, its apparent
Extension through time and space, is but
A single, eternal point broken
By some prism beyond our science
Into an insubstantial, spread fan
Of present, past and future. As is
Everything you see here.

WHITMAN: Impossible.
There, when I pinch him —

SWIMMER No. 1:   Hey, old man! —

WHITMAN: He jumps. Ow! And pinches back.
And what I feel for these rude youth
Around us is substantial. Even for you,
If you'd only relax. The swim didn't
Warm you up much. Or is that because,
According to you, the water's not water?

HOPKINS: I know Digby couldn't drown in it.

WHITMAN: Digby? Unless he had gills, he could.

HOPKINS: Digby Mackworth Dolben. My,
           Let me guess, Peter Doyle. The River
           Welland took him. At nineteen. I had
           Known him two years. Four years my younger,
           But that provided just enough distance
           To show how close we were. A convert,
           Like myself. Tenuous health. Sang
           No song of himself. In fact, once burned
           His hair off. Lit it with a candle.
           You wouldn't have approved of him. And
           He was the most beautiful young man
           I've ever seen.

WHITMAN: I would have approved.

HOPKINS: See that one wading out? I thought
           When I first saw him he was Digby.
           I had hoped it was he. Forever.
           But Digby had less flesh. As if
           The spirit crowded it off his bones.

WHITMAN: There you go again, setting the two
           Against each other like enemies. If these
           Are spiritual waters, they're also physical
           Ones, no illusion, and could drown your
           Friend again, or you for the first time.

HOPKINS: You're so enamored of your bulk — what
           Was it you wrote, "There is that lot
           Of me and all so luscious"? — you can't
           Admit your prized flesh has become
           A shadow.

WHITMAN: I can't, can't I? I'm
           Not a violent man, but if a dunking
           Can teach you this water's real, then

[87]

A dunking it'll be. Boys, it's time
For a little innocent American fun.

HOPKINS: In the name of . . .

CHORUS: Whoopee! We've got him.

WHITMAN: This is called, Holding Down Hopkins.

CHORUS: How long?

WHITMAN: Long enough for him to learn
The dangers of this swimming hole. He thinks
There's no harm can come to him here.
He has to be taught, for his own good health,
To respect water no matter where
It is.

SWIMMER No. 3: I think maybe he's learned
Enough respect. He's kicking pretty hard.

WHITMAN: Let him up then. We'll see if he wants
To quote poetry now.

SWIMMER No. 3:   You taught him
Too well. You won't even get him
To say his name for awhile.

WHITMAN: Quick!
Lift him out onto that flat rock.
Thank Eakins for an emergency bed,
Whether he intended one or not.
I'll just sit here next to him
Till he comes round. I've done this
Too much. I'm once again at Fredricksburg
And this young priest who loves me
But not well is my brother George
And many others.

HOPKINS: Then two times,
             And one timeless, merge here. I heard you.
             Barely. Your voice comes through a mist.
             You didn't quite flood me though you taught me
             How to choke in heaven. I don't know
             If I choked on water or it
             On me. If it was in my throat,
             I was in its. But I do know
             That if I'm a soldier in your Civil War,
             And thus American, you're also English,
             A Jesuit, in fact, who sits beside me
             On my deathbed. I said, "I am so
             Happy," then nothing else. Bridges
             Told me what your friend O'Conner
             Called you, in his book. A good grey
             Christ. Who is, of course, my lover.

WHITMAN: Bill went too far in praising me.
             Christ never nearly drowned a man.
             Though he did tempt some to walk on water.
             But if his words for me can help you
             Live with one who likes best
             The dress of the old Adam — though
             I do promise from time to time
             To put my clothes back on — I'm glad
             He said it.

HOPKINS: I close my eyes and that's
             My death. I open them, stand up,
             And that's my resurrection. You're the first
             Person my new eyes look on. Let
             My arm around your shoulder, draped
             In my Manley way, signify that.

WHITMAN: And let the two of us now formally
             Add ourselves to Tom Eakins' composition,
             His version of Eden. Shall we stand
             Like two blades, bucks, a certain

Tilt to our heads and jut to our hips
To show our pride in sex?

HOPKINS: Let's.

(All pose, the six young men as they did at the start, Hopkins and Whitman in such a way as not to fault Eakins' design.)

CODA

HE GOES TO A COSTUME PARTY
DRESSED AS GERARD MANLEY HOPKINS

The cassock doesn't quite fit, it's too loose
In the shoulders, and the white collar's more
Like a slipped halo, but that's all right, it
Makes me look thinner, and Hopkins, who ate
His meat smothered by a sauce of shadows,
Grew so thin over the years everyone since
Has been able to see clear through him to
Heaven.

        For a long time now I've been at work —
A friend jokes I must be at prayer — on a book
Of poems about Hopkins, many of which
He speaks or speaks in along with Bridges,
Felix Randal, even Walt Whitman. So when
The invitation came, I didn't have
To think at all. I'd be Hopkins. And am
Now, an unlikely drink in one hand, the other
Deep in the potato chips. A sign on my back
Advertises confessions, twenty-five cents.
I've had one taker so far, a lissome blonde
Who confessed she'd never made it
With a priest, especially a dead Jesuit,
And wondered if perhaps we couldn't offer
Ourselves up on that soft altar in the guestroom.
I tried to explain about virginity, his
Not mine, and propriety, a certain gesture
I owed his memory, or spirit even. But she
Was having none of it, was, after all, Dietrich
In *The Blue Angel,* from top hat to high-heeled shoes,
And I had once learned her famous torch song
By heart because I loved Lola-Lola's
Legs in black silk tights, and out of them.
                                 So
In we went, shutting the door as a mummy
Smoking a cigarette and Dorothy Lamour in
Road to Rio passed by, and tripped the lock.

Glory be to God for dappled things, like hips
The white grip of elastic still marks, a mons
Fur rides electrically, and, look, see, there, ah,
The achieve of, the mastery of, a mouth. What would
Dear, hidden Hopkins say about this spread
Of Nature, fold, fallow, and plough, the wholly
Holy holey beautiful, hard prod of breasts?
Once said, "I think there is no one can admire
Beauty of the body more than I do."
So say it aloud. "A talker, are you?"
"That was Hopkins. Only he saw more men's
Bodies than women's. Lots. Was eloquent on brawn
And thew." Her thigh muscle ripples. "Not, I'll not
Untwist, slack they may be, these legs, love-legs,
Knot of them, inscape of outriding
Joy." "More Hopkins?" Her belly shines
Like shook foil. "Sort of." I touch the fine
Brown spot on her shoulder her birth gave her.
"Thisness," I say. "Huh?" "It's his word. It means
The sign that means you are, and are no other."
She licks my neck, singly, in answer. Soon it's time
For the rolling level underneath us steady air
And we swing off on a bow-bend, pride, plume, and act here
Buckle! And the fire that breaks from us then, a billion
Times told lovelier, O my Chevalass, as we fall
Gall ourselves, and kiss, in carnal heaven,
Two worlds, like no and yes, impossibly allied.

That was then. Now she's leggily atop
The piano, one knee cupped in her hands,
The classic's classic shot, surrounded by
Berliners, and I think she's singing to me,
Dacey playing Hopkins playing Emil Jannings
Playing Professor Immanuel Rath playing
The fool. *Ich bin von Kopf bis Fuss.* What I
Want to know is, Who's playing Dacey, and Why?
I'll go home tonight and strip down as far

As I can, and maybe meet my part's actor
In the dark, but for now, let me be Gerard,
And him in love, and us holding up the bar.

SOME NOTES ON THE POEMS

The two editor's notes are fabrications, although the quotation in the one for "Angel Hopkins" is genuine, as are all the quotations used as epigraphs or in the text. "The Peaches" is based on an actual incident, though all the dialogue is invented; "The Sitting," on the other hand, is not so based (Wooldridge used a photograph of Hopkins in making his portrait). Hopkins' ether-induced dream derives from a dream of a patient of William James. Three other dreams presented in the book (in "Mater Investida," "Hopkins to Bridges," and "Essays in Criticism") are inventions, while the dream in "A Simple Garden Ladder" has its source in a photograph accompanying a review—in a *Saturday Review* I can no longer identify — of an avant-garde ballet. Hopkins' nickname was indeed "Skin." And Hopkins himself must be held responsible for the reference in "The Sitting" to his heart and vitals as all shaggy with the whitest hair. The prose letter to Bridges is an invention, as is the Kerr book mentioned in it, though the gist of Kerr's book was suggested by Charles Williams. The only record of a relationship between Felix Randal and Hopkins is the poem by Hopkins. The coda, like so much of the book, mixes fact and fiction: the fact is my costume, the fiction is Marlene Dietrich. A complete sorting out of the factual and fictitious threads would, of course, require a long and tedious essay. And I must confess that in some instances I no longer remember if the material was invented or found. I do remember, though, that a line in "The Peaches" comes from a poem by Donald Justice; I retain the line because it fits so perfectly in the mouth of Hopkins.

Philip Dacey

ACKNOWLEDGEMENTS

Certain poems in this book first appeared in the following periodicals, whose permission to reprint is gratefully acknowledged: *American Review*: "Hopkins to Bridges: From the Secret Correspondence"; *The Beloit Poetry Journal*: "The Bloomery" (originally entitled "Inspired Iron"); *Carolina Quarterly*: "The Sitting"; *The Literary Review*: "A Dream of Hopkins"; *Memphis State Review*: "The Man of Capernaum"; *The Mickle Street Review*: "Gerard Manley Hopkins Meets Walt Whitman in Heaven"; *Michigan Quarterly Review*: "Skin"; *Nimrod*: "Angel Hopkins"; *Poet Lore*: "The Device," "Nomen Numen," "A Work in Progress"; *Poetry Northwest*: "Remembering Adam and Eve"; *Victorian Poetry*: "The Peaches," "Comic Hopkins" (an earlier version of this poem appeared in *Gravida*). "Essays in Criticism" reprinted by permission of Kansas State University, copyright © *Kansas Quarterly*, 1981. "A Simple Garden Ladder" reprinted with permission from *The North American Review*, copyright © 1978 by the University of Northern Iowa. "Hopkins Under Ether" reprinted by permission of editor of *Poetry* and copyrighted in 1978 by The Modern Poetry Association. "Hopkins to His Jesuit Superior" and "Mater Investida" reprinted from *The Carleton Miscellany*, copyrighted by Carleton College, May 22, 1978. "The Sleep" reprinted from Summer 1976 *Prairie Schooner* by permission of the University of Nebraska Press. Copyright © 1976 University of Nebraska Press. "He Goes to a Costume Party Dressed as Gerard Manley Hopkins" reprinted by permission from *The Hudson Review*, Vol. XXXI, No. 1 (Spring, 1978). Copyright © 1978 by Philip Dacey. "The Sleep" appeared, without a G. M. Hopkins connection, in *The Boy Under the Bed*, Copyright © 1981 The Johns Hopkins University Press.

The author also gratefully acknowledges the receipt of a Pushcart Prize (1977) for "The Sleep"; a First Prize in Poetry from *Prairie Schooner* (Vol. 50, 1976-77) for the same poem; a First Prize in the Gerard Manley Hopkins Memorial Sonnet Competition (1977) for the first part of "Hopkins Under Ether"; a First Award, 1980-81, from *Kansas Quarterly* for "Essays in Criticism"; and a Fellowship for Artists from the Bush Foundation of Saint Paul, Minnesota, which was granted specifically to effect the completion of this book.

Special thanks go to David Jauss, who contributed mightily from start to finish by his encouragement and astute criticism. Thanks, too, to Carl Sutton, whose good will toward this work meant a lot. More than thanks to Florence, who, as my wife, was a full partner in this endeavor.

COLOPHON

†

*GERARD MANLEY HOPKINS
MEETS WALT WHITMAN IN HEAVEN
AND OTHER POEMS*
was hand-printed in an edition of nine hundred copies
at Penmaen Press during the summer of 1982.
Three hundred books were case-bound, and six hundred
were paper-bound. The binding was done at the
Stinehour Press in Lunenburg, Vermont.

Michael McCurdy designed & printed the book.
He set the Linotype Times New Roman with the
assistance of John Kristensen.
The paper is 70lb. Mohawk Superfine Text.

Seventy-five copies of the hardcover were numbered
and signed by the poet and artist.